DAZZLING DESIGNS
Coloring Book

by
Koichi Sato

DOVER PUBLICATIONS, INC.
Mineola, New York

Publisher's Note

This coloring book is the latest product of the fertile visual imagination of the graphic artist Koichi Sato. Untethered to the coloring conventions dictated by representations of actual objects, these images present unlimited possibilities to the colorist. It is impossible to make a "wrong" choice. Use whatever scheme you wish, and the finished design will be uniquely your own. No one else—not even the original artist—will have seen it the way you have!

Copyright

Copyright © 1998 by Koichi Sato
All rights reserved under Pan American and International copyright conventions.

Published in Canada by General Publishing Company, Ltd., 30 Lesmill Road, Don Mills, Toronto, Ontario.

Bibliographical Note

Dazzling Designs Coloring Book is a new work, first published by Dover Publications, Inc., in 1998.

DOVER *Pictorial Archive* SERIES

This book belongs to the Dover Pictorial Archive Series. You may use the designs and illustrations for graphics and crafts applications, free and without special permission, provided that you include no more than ten in the same publication or project. (For permission for additional use, please write to: Permissions Department, Dover Publications, Inc., 31 East 2nd Street, Mineola, N.Y. 11501.)

However, republication or reproduction of any illustration by any other graphic service, whether it be in a book or in any other design resource, is strictly prohibited.

International Standard Book Number: 0-486-40031-X

Manufactured in the United States of America
Dover Publications, Inc., 31 East 2nd Street, Mineola, N. Y. 11501

1

2

3

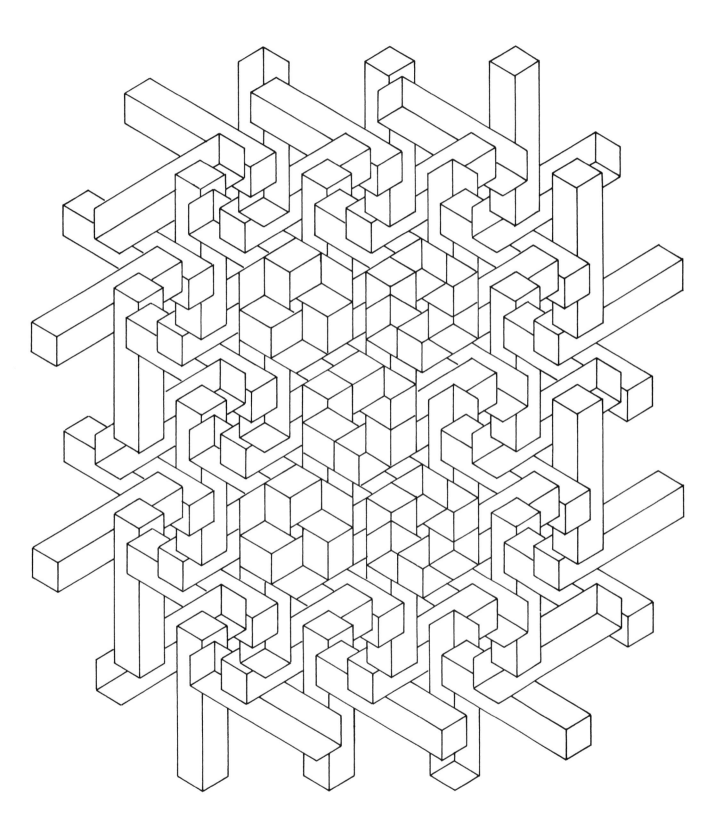

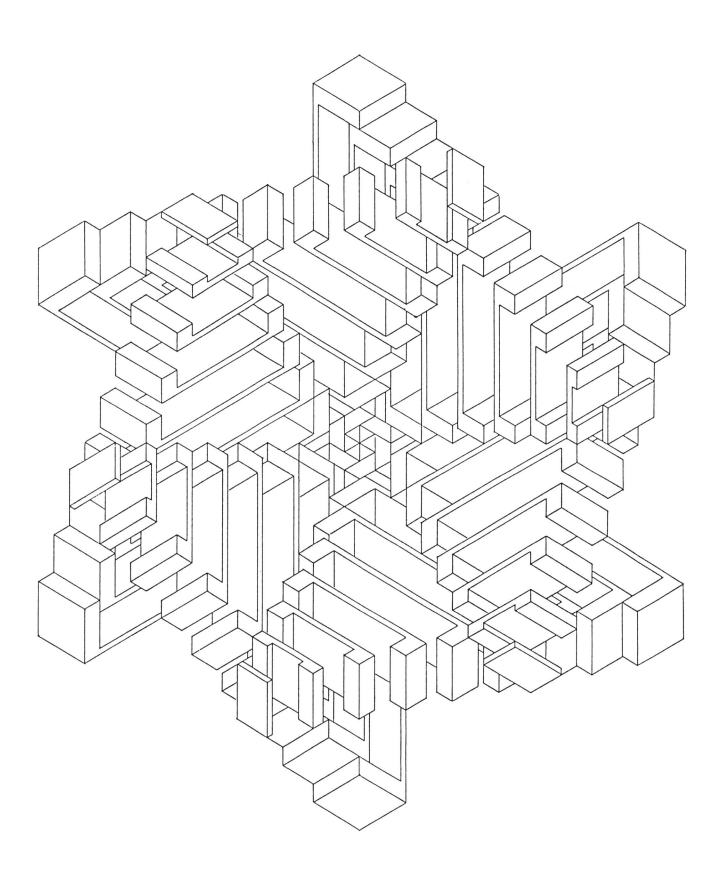

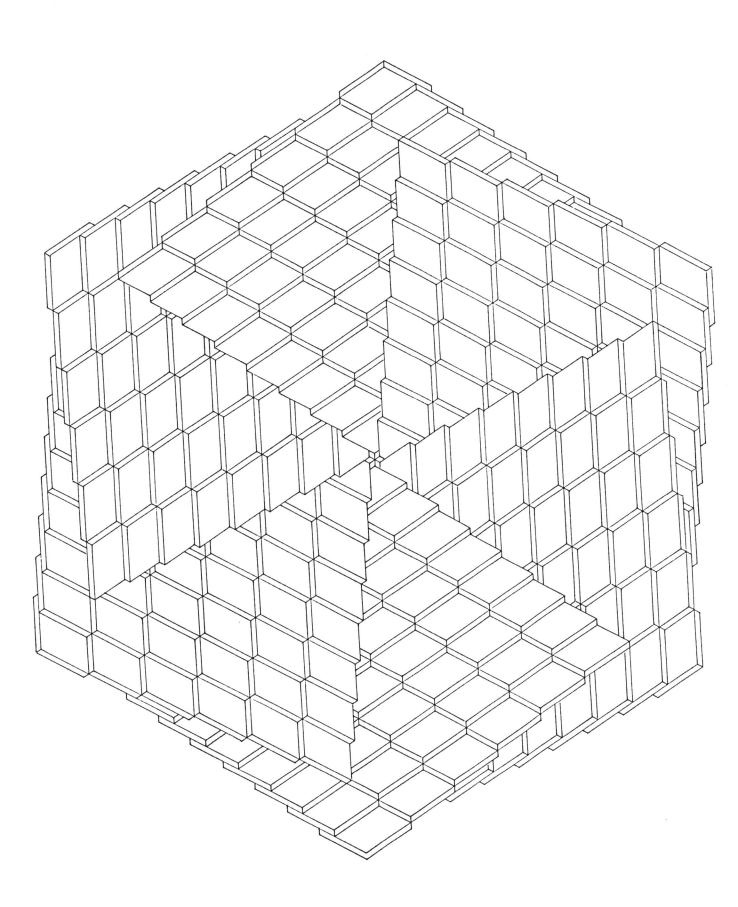

9

14

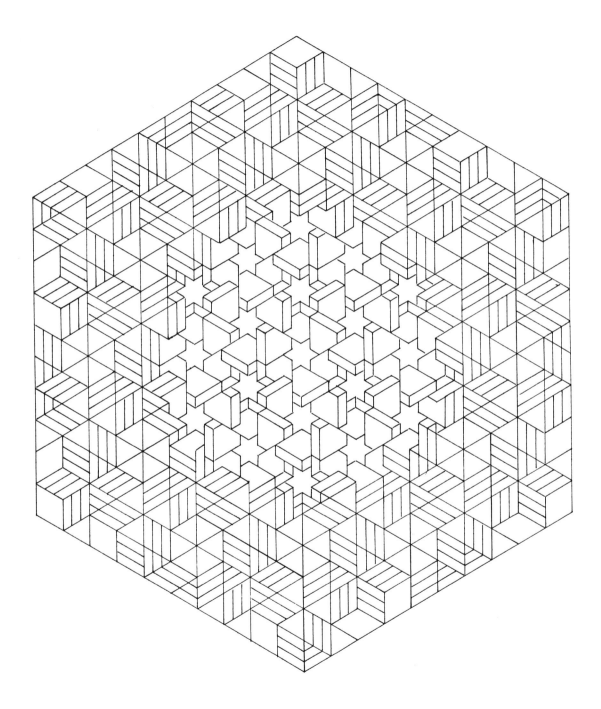

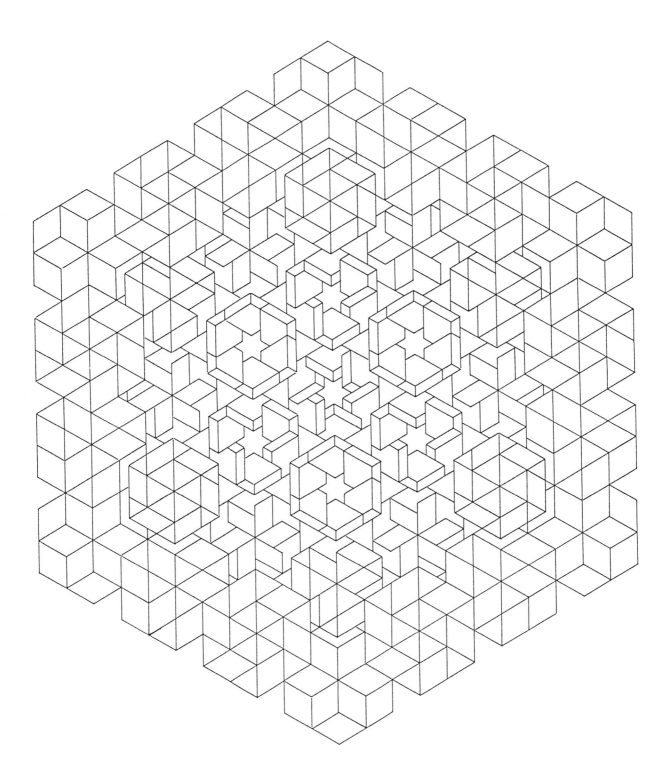

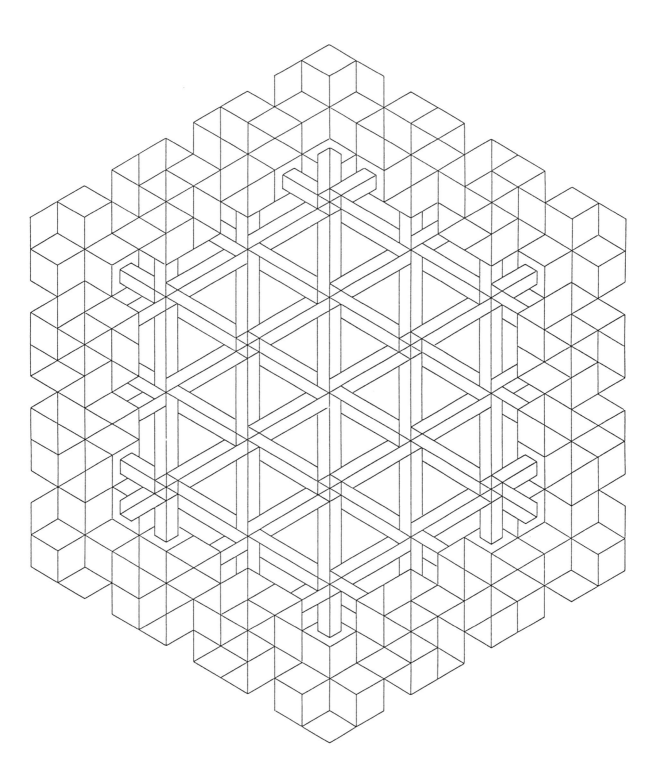

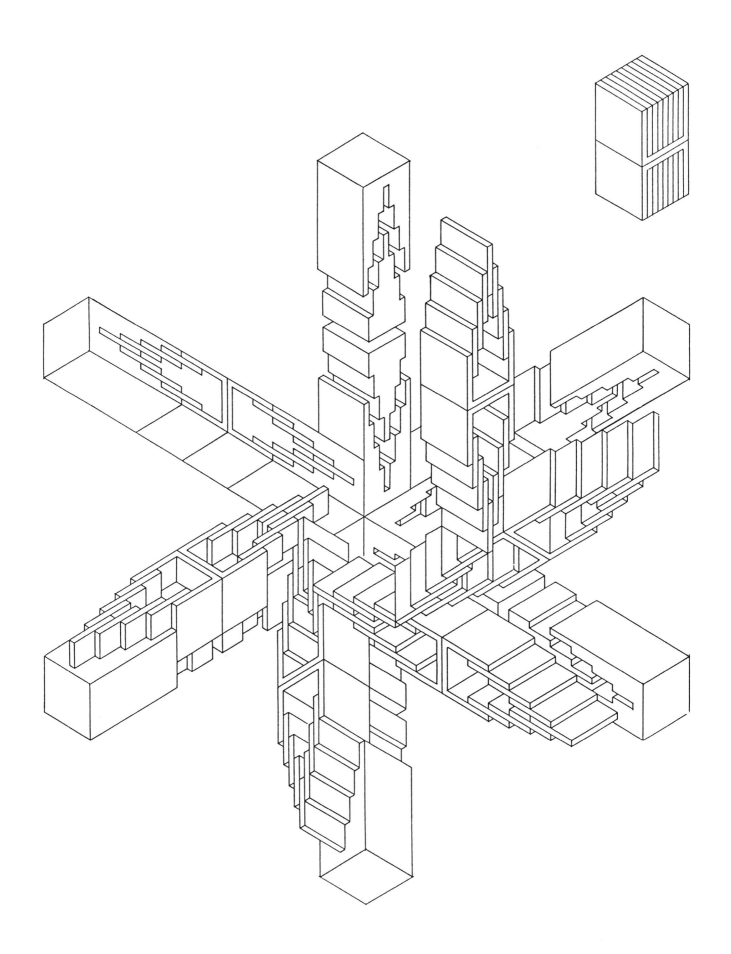

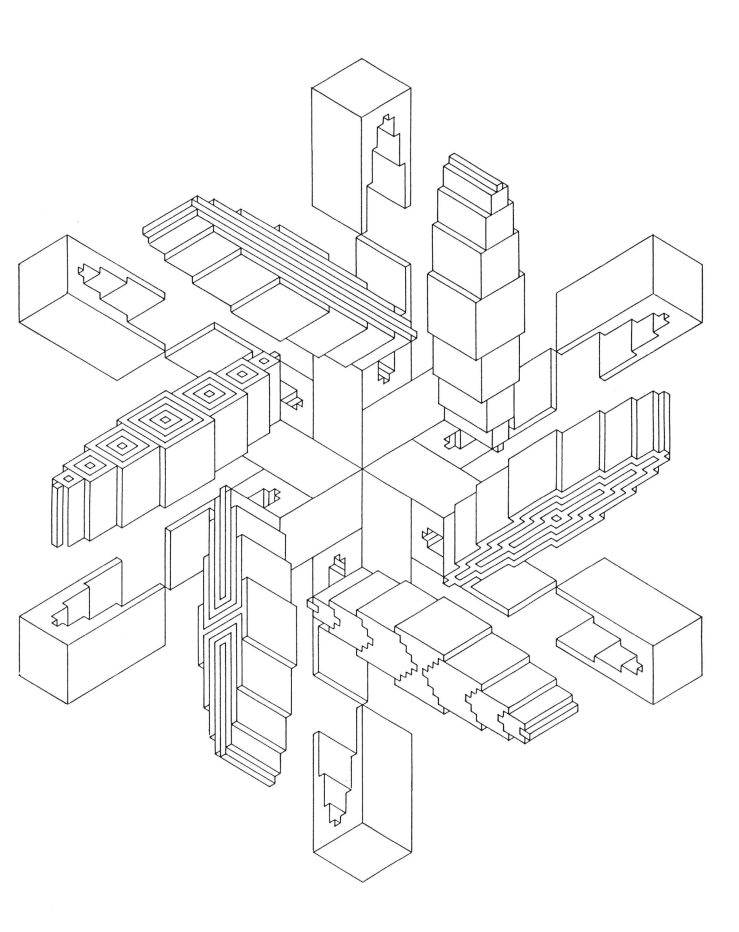